Travels With
My Sketchbook

Michael Foreman

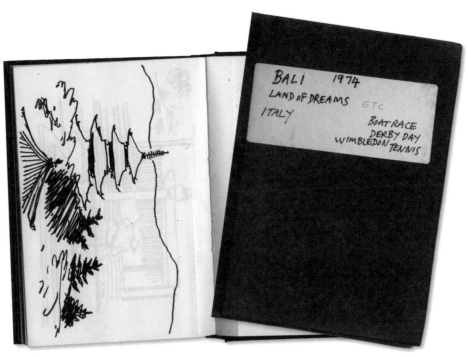

t

templar publishing

*To my sons, Mark, Ben and Jack,
the 'sonshine of my life'*

A TEMPLAR BOOK

First published in the UK in 2017 by Templar Publishing,
part of the Bonnier Publishing Group,
The Plaza, 535 King's Road, London, SW10 0SZ
www.templarco.co.uk
www.bonnierpublishing.com

The Publishers would like to thank the following for permission to reproduce
illustrative material: Walker Books Ltd (pp. 82–3, illustrations from *Mia's Story*);
Andersen Press (pp. 84–7, illustrations from *Wonder Goal!*); Pavilion Books
(pp. 13, 25, 44, 68, 75, illustrations from *A Life in Pictures*).

1 3 5 7 9 10 8 6 4 2

ISBN 978 - 1 - 78370 - 472 - 9

The illustrations were created using pen, pencil and watercolours

Written by Michael Foreman
Edited by Kate Baker
Designed by Helen Chapman

Printed in Malaysia

Contents

Drawing the World

I was born above the village shop run by our mum. We had no books but my head was filled with the stories told by the flood of soldiers and sailors who frequented our shop during the Second World War. My favourite stories were those told by the Americans; tales of cowboys and skyscrapers and grizzly bears. I realized there was a big world out there, and I was a little boy who wanted to see it . . .

As the war ended, exotic fruits and boxes of dates with palm trees and pyramids on the labels began arriving in our shop. I wanted to see where these wonders came from. I never imagined that drawing would be my golden ticket.

The shop was at the heart of the village and inspired my book War Boy

When I illustrated my first book – *The General* – in 1961, I was still at art school. I hadn't been anywhere, so I set the story in the landscape of my childhood – the Suffolk fishing village of Pakefield. One of the early scenes depicts the beach. My brother, 'Pud', owned one of the fishing boats on the beach, his father-in-law owned the ice cream stall on the clifftop and the churchyard contains generations of Foremans.

Although the setting is very local, the story reflected the worldwide fear, particularly among young people, of nuclear war. There was a finger-on-the-button face-off between Russia and the West. The rest of the world waited and hoped for peace.

illustrated by
Michael Foreman

50 ANNIVERSARY EDITION YEARS

A Celebration of Peace and Beauty

The General

Janet Charters

Above: Recently, the fiftieth anniversary of The General *was celebrated with publications in both Russia and the West*

Right: The sea, the lifeblood of our town, joined our little island to the rest of the wide, wide world (illustration from The General)

11

The American Dream

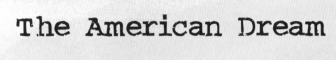

I graduated from the Royal College of Art in 1963 with a Travel Scholarship to America – the land of my childhood dreams.

The first glimpse of the skyline of Manhattan from the back of my yellow cab was a thrill I could never forget. It is an experience I have been lucky enough to repeat many times and the buzz just keeps on buzzing.

Sunset Boulevard – one of the world's urban joys. A slow, serpentine evening drive through the whole gamut of LA style. We drive east to west – it's like driving into the sunset.

I criss-crossed the vast country by Greyhound Bus, east to west and from Canada down to Mexico. One sour note was the racial segregation, which still existed, unbelievably, in the Southern States. Black people were not allowed to sit at the front of the bus. Naturally, the back of the bus became the place for me.

'Sleepy time down South' – back of the bus, Atlanta, 1963

Tijuana, Mexican Border, 1963

The only time our mum shut her shop was on Sunday afternoons, when her favourite treat was to take me on a 'Magical Mystery Coach Tour'. It was magical, but not very 'mysterious' as it always included a couple of hours at Great Yarmouth Pleasure Beach. I found many reminders of those golden Sunday afternoons in the coastal towns of America.

New Haven, Long Island Sound

Coney Island, New York

Since that first visit in 1963, I have returned to the US fifty or sixty times. I found myself a wonderful New York artist's agent, John Locke, who had represented some of my illustrator heroes from the golden age of American illustration in the 1940s and 50s.

I became a roving illustrator – back and forth from London to New York and Chicago doing magazine drawings all over the US. From oil refineries and pipelines in Alaska and Mexico to American football, baseball and the Indianapolis five hundred motor race. I also worked in Denmark and France doing animation and political cartoons for the British press. Travel became a way of life.

Above: Alaska

Below: Oil pipelines in Mexico

Down Highway One to Mexico –
One of the World's Great Road Trips

San Francisco, a relaxed and gentle start to the journey
south. A cosmopolitan and unique city where hills and
cable cars 'climb halfway to the stars'.

Highway One rolls down the Pacific coast of California, through the hill pastures of San Luis Obispo County, then cuts across to the bay of Santa Barbara. Thickets of motel and drive-in and take-out signs herald the jungle of billboards and neon to come on the last haul to Los Angeles.

The Coast Highway, Big Sur

Malibu — the Mecca of surfers. A straggle of wooden beach houses and fish restaurants. Oil rigs stand like wading birds in the bay. The Hollywood sign fades in the hills and a flourish of birds flicker like closing credits across the setting sun.

Muscle Beach — jogging, surfing, skateboarding, yoga and rollerskating.

Disneyland — overtaken and eclipsed by the real-life lunacy outside.

The great aisle of palms on the cliffs of Santa Monica

During my first trip in 1963, I went on the typical tourist bus tour of the 'Homes of the Stars' in the Hollywood Hills. In 1968, I was commissioned by the British magazine, Nova, to draw some of those glamorous places.

Many of the old film stars were long gone – replaced by the new stars of rock 'n' roll. It was still a thrill for the little boy from Pakefield to visit the places where the stars of my Saturday morning dreams at the cinema had lived.

House of movie star Tyrone Power in the Hollywood Hills where I stayed, 1968

la Jolla, just north of the Mexican border. The American Dream of a small town. Palm-lined streets and well-lined pockets. The trees are so high they appear to grow downwards like drips from the sky. 85% of Californians live within 30 miles of the sea. Young and old grow more reptilian, throwing Darwin into reverse, leading man's slow swim to the last great sunset.

Monument Valley engulfed in snow

Land of Contrasts

In 1993 I was researching a book about Native American legends and
my family and I were driving through the land of the Navajo in Arizona
– long straight empty roads across vast landscapes. Monument Valley
engulfed us in a sudden sandstorm and the following morning we awoke
to snow! The red world of the day before was now a white wonderland.

Navajo shepherd, Monument Valley

DINOSAUR TRACKS

The precious prints are looked after by a few young Navajo, armed with yellow plastic brooms to keep the sand away. One of the Navajo, David, told us that one of the best specimens had been chiselled out and stolen. The area was unfenced. The Navajo need more than yellow plastic brooms to protect their windblown inheritance.

*Jack and Ben and the dinosaur print,
near Tuba City, Arizona, 1993*

The Ancient Land of the Aztecs

Although I crossed the Mexican border a few times during my first visit to the US, it was several years later that I visited Mexico proper. I travelled Highway One down the Californian coast and the Pacific coast of Mexico and on to the drama and colour of Mexico City, then to the ancient wonders of the Yucatan Peninsula, drawing the spectacular ruins of the Olmec, Aztec and Mayan temples.

Mexican border town

Santa Clara Pueblo, New Mexico – famous for pottery – many of the most famous potters are women

On a later trip, I followed the winding course of the Rio Grande from the Rocky Mountains down to the Gulf of Mexico – researching the Native American culture in the ancient Pueblos.

Temple of the plumed serpent God, Kukulkan, Chichen-Itza, Yukatan

A Siberian Sketchbook

In 1970 I was commissioned to make drawings of the World Fair in Osaka, Japan. Rather than fly straight there, I felt it would be more of an adventure to try to go by train through Europe, Russia and Siberia on the fabled Trans-Siberian Express. Then, maybe spend my fee returning home around the other side of the world by boat and plane.

Friday, 3rd July, 1970
9.40am – Slid out of liverpool Street Station into the world. I have left here on numerous occasions to visit my family in Suffolk, just three hours away. Today my ticket is from london to Nadhodka, over three weeks away.

Saturday 4th July

On reaching the Berlin Wall, the train is searched at 4am with dogs. Each carriage is locked at both ends. If there is a restaurant car, it is impossible to get to it. Fortunately my companions, two Buddhist monks and a Russian from the London Trade Delegation, have all three been to Fortnum and Mason and have well-stocked hampers. I eat well.

Sunday 5th July

Spent three days in Moscow. Wandered down tree-lined and litter-free streets, dotted with beautiful churches, quiet backstreets and leafy gardens.

27

Wednesday 8th July
On the Trans-Siberian Express. Travelled all day through rolling country, small woods and hayricks. It's now 8.30pm. There has been nothing but forest for the past hour . . .

Thursday 9th July
Same forest and mile after mile of purple lupins. Despite the monotony, my face was pressed to the window. Having read Pasternak, I knew that soon there would be 'The Sign' . . . And there it was! The sign! A stone obelisk with ASIA carved into it. We crossed into Asia.

"'It'll come soon,' he murmured . . . "The signpost they talk about, on the frontier of Asia and Europe." – Dr Zhivago, Boris Pasternak

Friday 10th July

The train travels fast across vast grasslands with groups of big firs and butterflies. Folk songs dash from radios installed in all parts of the train. The whole thing becomes even more dreamlike. We pass a train loaded with tanks and soldiers sitting on them, waving, close to the Mongolian border.

More days and nights of sweeping hills and forest. We see girls with flowers in their hair and around their necks, similarly decorating cows with garlands. It no longer matters if the train is fast or stopped, we are suspended, lost in this long long bedroom, with mile after mile of wild flowers for wallpaper.

29

I had two pre-arranged stopovers, in Novosibirsk, Central Siberia, and one in Irkutsk on the shores of Lake Baikal, near the Mongolian border. Lake Baikal – the deepest lake in the world. The lake was so deep and so cold it was like standing in front of an open fridge.

I stopped at a small wayside museum containing lots of stuffed birds and animals of the area including a moose. I hadn't realized that moose were native to both North America and Siberia. Being so far behind the Iron Curtain (possibly, by now, nearer to the US than to Moscow) and standing next to this rather sad flea-bitten moose, the Cold War seemed even more ridiculous. My picture book, *Moose*, (representing the common man trapped between threatening 'superpowers') was published a year later in 1971.

lovely old churches were being carefully repaired and were full of plastic flowers. The fields around were full of real ones. lakes were like fallen bits of sky.

We left Irkutsk at midnight, now pulled by a giant steam locomotive, so suddenly, the fresh air of Siberia was full of soot. We were adrift in Asia, pulled slowly over the rolling Steppe towards the Pacific ocean. There was no wind. The flowers in the fields didn't dance and red flags, bleached pink, hung motionless.

The occasional stops at small stations had a garden fete atmosphere. Everyone leapt down from the trains to buy drinks, sweets, tobacco etc. from stalls. A toot from the engine brought the passengers scurrying aboard from their brief walk and chat in the sun.

2km north of China. Suddenly it's like another country. None of the trees are straight, like trees on Chinese ceramics. We arrive at Nadhodka, the end of the line, and take the boat to Japan.

The World Fair

The World Fair in Osaka was just a World Fair.
Sixty million visitors, two thousand million dollars
spent, seventy-six nations trying to out-do each other.
It did not detain me long. I wanted to see the country.

I travelled on the then state-of-the-art 'Bullet Train',
Japan's marvellously efficient rail system – you don't
check your watch to see if the train is on time, you
check the train to see if your watch is correct. I
criss-crossed the country to ancient temples, saw the
wonder of Mount Fuji and knew that I would be back.

Above: People of all nations cool their feet,
The World Fair, Osaka, 1970

Below: Bullet train and Mount Fuji, 1983

I took the long way home, around the back of the world – from Tokyo to Hong Kong, Manila to Vietnam, to Singapore, across the Pacific, stopping off in Tahiti, Fiji and Hawaii, and then back across America.

It was the height of the Vietnam War and, flying in over the countryside, round brown patches in the forest became round brown pools as they spread into the paddy fields. Bomb craters. A sudden burst of sun made them shine. Vietnam looked like it had been blitzed by giant silver dollars – and I suppose it had.

Planes disgorged wounded and, amid the mayhem, a small girl held up two fingers of peace.

Flying over the Mekong Delta, Vietnam

33

Land of the Rising Sun

In 1972, I returned to Japan to work on a book about its traditional crafts. It was a wonderful opportunity to see much more of the country because many of the artists we visited had the good sense to live in remote and beautiful areas – some on islands off the mainland.

I have always admired the Japanese use of watercolour and this trip influenced my work even more. The travels and sketches were invaluable when I illustrated a collection of Japanese legends in *The Shining Princess* by Eric Quayle. We were privileged to watch the greatest craftspeople at work; potters, weavers, stencil-cutters, paper makers, a swordsmith, artists in bamboo, lacquer and wood, and the art of the kimono.

Above: Flying over Mt Fuji

Below: Miyajima, the Inland Sea

Shoji Hamada worked with Bernard Leach in St Ives in the 1920s, so I was keen to meet him. He lived 120 kilometres east of Tokyo in the pottery village of Mashiko. I watched him deftly decorating pots with a variety of bamboo brushes. "Sometimes people say I paint quickly," he said, "but I am not quick. Each brush stroke takes sixty years plus one second."

Before I left, Hamada placed two rows of pots along his garden path and invited me to choose one. A tiny, shiny green tree frog leapt onto a simple dish and hopped off into the undergrowth. I picked that one.

"A quiet pot for a quiet man," said Shoji Hamada.

In Kurikoma Valley, 84-year-old Mrs Ayano Chiba grew hemp in fields by the river. It grew 1.5 metres high, much taller than she was. She harvested it and wove it into long lengths of cloth on an ancient loom.

Ayano also grew 'ai' (indigo) which she used to dye the cloth. She decorated this with stencils using flour paste as a resist. She sunk the dyed cloth in the river and the fish ate the flour resist leaving the design clear in the blue background. She planted, grew, spun, wove, dyed – and the fish added the finishing touches.

35

Thirty-Six Views of Mount Fuji

The next time I went to Japan it was to draw Mount Fuji, thirty-six times. A hundred years before, Japanese artist Hokusai had produced his famous series of prints 'Thirty-Six Views of Mount Fuji'. I was asked to do a modern series.

At first, I tried to find the exact locations from which Hokusai had viewed the mountain. Some views were from Tokyo itself but, of course, much has changed since Hokusai's time. Tokyo has become a city of skyscrapers and freeways. The high-rise urban sprawl spreads across the central plain of Japan to the foot of Fuji itself blocking out many of the famous views.

Then I learnt that Hokusai had re-arranged nature. Geographical studies show that he could not have seen Fuji from some of the viewpoints of his pictures. He also left out unnecessary detail and things he didn't like, and exaggerated things he did like. Good man.

Armed with new resolve, new Japanese paints and brushes, I set off. Not quite in the great man's footsteps, but by the wonderful Bullet Train.

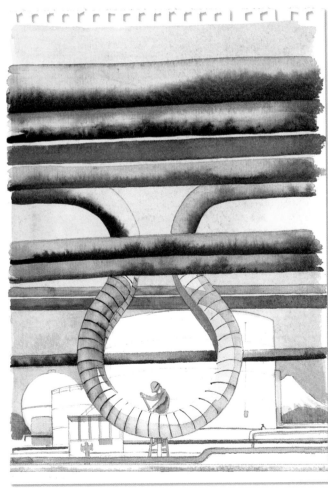

Hokusai was of peasant stock and served a long apprenticeship illustrating 'yellow back' novels or 'penny dreadfuls' – the pulp fiction of his day. He said he was 'driven to draw' at the age of six and worked constantly for almost seventy years as an illustrator of literature of every kind and as a recorder of the Japan of his day.

I felt closer to Hokusai than to any other artist in history.

Right: Roofs echoing cloud-shrouded Fuji

Below right: Board meeting of oil executives at health spa

Below: Fuji tennis club

A Norwegian Journey
– Top of the World to the Bottom of the Sea

I have been fortunate to illustrate myths and legends from many parts of the world. In 1985, I was commissioned to draw on the oil rigs in the North Sea off the coast of Norway and witnessed the wild power of the elements and the enterprise of the people – as evident now as in the days of the Norse Sagas.

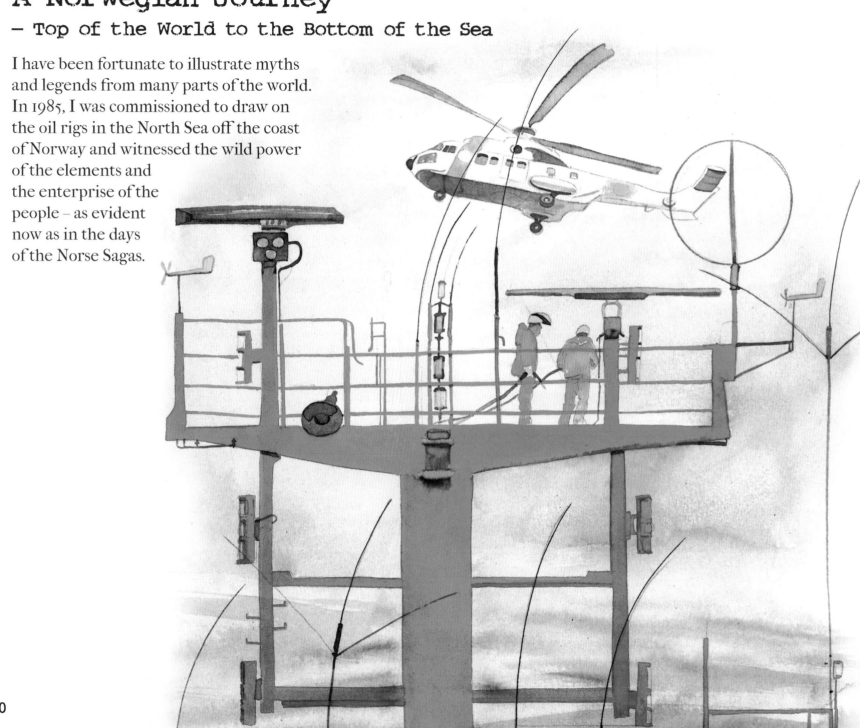

We continue down through the heavy breathing pipes and bowels of the vast platform, to the foot of one of the legs – 150 metres below the surface. All is calm. There is no sense of the storm above. There is a feeling of detachment, like a monk's cell below an unholy cathedral.

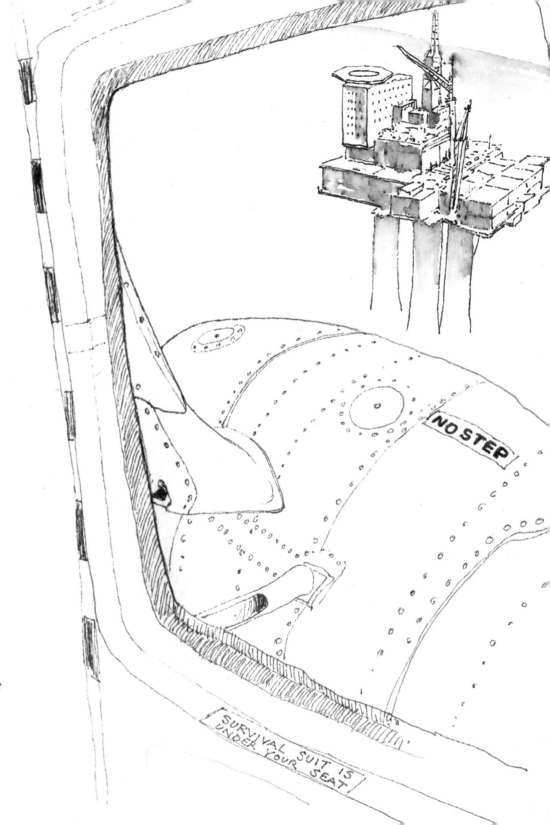

Above: On the flight back, the helicopter is full of men in giant survival suits and one diminutive lady doing a needlepoint of Viking children

Right: Helicopter leaving oil platform

The Northern Star

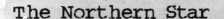

When I had finished the drawings on the rigs, I wanted to go further north, into the Arctic. I wanted snow. I wanted to see reindeer!

The 'Northern Star', part of the 'Coastal Express' fleet, was an old boat with a friendly feel. It was like a local bus. It took me up the coast of Norway and into the Arctic circle, making many stops on the way, loading and unloading goods and animals.

We set sail at 11pm and make two or three stops during the rolling night. From my bunk I see people get on and off in pouring rain. A cow is hoisted high over a wet moon, or was it a dream?

Strings of wooden houses sit along the edge of the sea, with towering dark mountains rising sheer behind them. Glacial streams tumble through backyards. Everything moves on this ship. There are waves in my wine. My chair is sliding about with me on it. I have a mouthful of coffee as I pass by the cup. There is a storm warning so we put into Trondheim. May be stuck for days. I decide to jump ship.

Into the Wilderness

I caught the bus to Kautokeino in the Arctic Circle at the top of Norway. There was deep snow everywhere. The low sun glinted golden off the packed snow road surface. It felt like I was following the 'yellow brick road' to the land of Oz.

A local guide, Mikel Triumf, agreed to take me to the reindeer herds in the north. Mikel was five feet square and looked like he could cope with anything. We were joined by Joachim, a young German silversmith. Joachim was hitchhiking to Kathmandu in the 1960s, but wandered off the Hippy trail, as you do, found himself in Lapland and never left.

7am – It's 38 degrees below and we're off, driving into white haze. There is no horizon, no colour in the sky, no ground. Just blank white, and then the reindeer. A blank, white world, like an untouched page in a sketchbook.

We set off for the wilderness early in the morning, across frozen lakes and rivers following an old 'winter way', marked by tall twigs stuck in the snow fifty yards apart. In the evening we arrived at a group of snow-covered huts where we spent the night dining on Maryland cookies and reindeer meat.

The Lapps began to tell stories. The old stories. The 'Changeling' stories are very strong here. Every Lapp baby has a silver bauble hanging in the cot to keep the people from the 'Underworld' away. Despite their dose of Christianity, the older Lapps still have ancient sacred places where ancestors' good and bad spirits reside.

When I go outside, after too much coffee, I worry I might get rooted to the spot by a frozen arc of pee.

The next day the big sled reindeer had to be separated from the rest before the whole herd started on its Spring migration to Summer pasture at the coast. They must be separated before the big move because once the herd starts off nothing can stop them, and they are needed to pull the supply sleds.

Lapps zoomed off in different directions gathering scattered groups of reindeer and driving them toward the main herd. Then the whole herd surged like a tide, a brown racing wave breaking over the white hills.

46

As each Lapp picked out a sled reindeer he tried to lasso it – sometimes while still travelling at speed on his skidoo. When he was successful he would plunge into the snow and bring the galloping reindeer to an abrupt stop. Then there was a tug-of-war until the reindeer was secured to a sled.

They worked in pairs. The man and wife team seemed the best. They were all enjoying their day. Not sure how the reindeer felt about it. Two were killed for meat.

The long journey back to Kautokeino was leisurely. I was reluctant to leave the wilderness. The night bus to Alta was waved to a stop by a lone figure at the roadside. It was Joachim. He held up a silver ball on a chain. He had made it. He asked me to hang it in the cot of my baby, Ben, to ward off the people from the Underworld. The kindness of strangers is one of the joys of travel.

48

In the Footsteps of Marco Polo

At school we learned of Marco Polo. I pictured the young Marco growing up in Venice, surrounded by all the scents of spices arriving from the Orient. The accounts of his travels made him a hero in my imagination, at least the equal of Robin Hood. As life turned out, I went to virtually all of the countries to which Marco travelled long before I went to Sherwood Forest.

I had made the usual art student visits to Paris and Amsterdam, but Venice, in 1960, was the first really foreign place I saw. No longer the Northern light of home – but a new, dancing light. I wanted to follow in Marco Polo's footsteps but, because of the geo-politics of the time, there were some borders I couldn't cross. I had to visit some countries one by one, returning to the UK between trips.

Above: In 1271, the Polos set sail on a journey which would last twenty-four years. The first stage was across the Mediterranean, past Athens to Acre. Then to Jerusalem to obtain holy oil from Christ's sepulchre as a gift for the Great Khan

Left: Piazza San Marco, Venice – frequently flooded by the Adriaic and constanty by tourists

The Holy Land and the Land of the Pharaohs

When I was nine years old at school we used to listen to Old Testament plays on the radio. They used to start after school dinners on Monday and last about forty minutes. They were brilliant, with a large cast of actors and exciting sound effects. Because it was radio, it was very real. When the play finished we had to paint what we had just heard. The best lesson of the week!

Many years later, in 1980, I was asked to draw the same scenes again for a collection of Old Testament stories retold by Peter Dickinson. The book was called 'The City of Gold'. It was a pleasure to delve back into the old sketchbooks to capture the atmosphere of the Holy Land.

Above: The Dome of the Rock, on Mount Moriah, Jerusalem. The traditional site of Abraham's sacrificial altar for Isaac; the launching place for Muhammad's leap into Heaven. His footprint can still be seen – as can hairs from his beard

Right: Head of Ramesses II and shepherd boy, Thebes

Take to the Nile for Upper Egypt and see the wonders of the Valley of the Kings, the Temples of Karnak, the Colossi of Memnon, all the way to Aswan and the Rock Temple of Ramesses II at Abu Simbel.

Cairo is one of my favourite cities. The weekly camel market, beyond unpromising railway tracks, is a scene bursting from the Bible. All is noise, shouts, snorting camels and bleating sheep. Small boys ride donkeys, Biblical style, way back on the haunches, at speed, steering with a stick.

Above: The remains of the Temple of Ptah at Memphis, dominated by the most ancient stone building in the world – the Step Pyramid at Sakkara

Left: Sweeping sand from the foot of the Sphinx – a full time job. Cairo presses right up to the feet of the Pyramids, but behind them is the vast empty expanse of the Libyan Desert

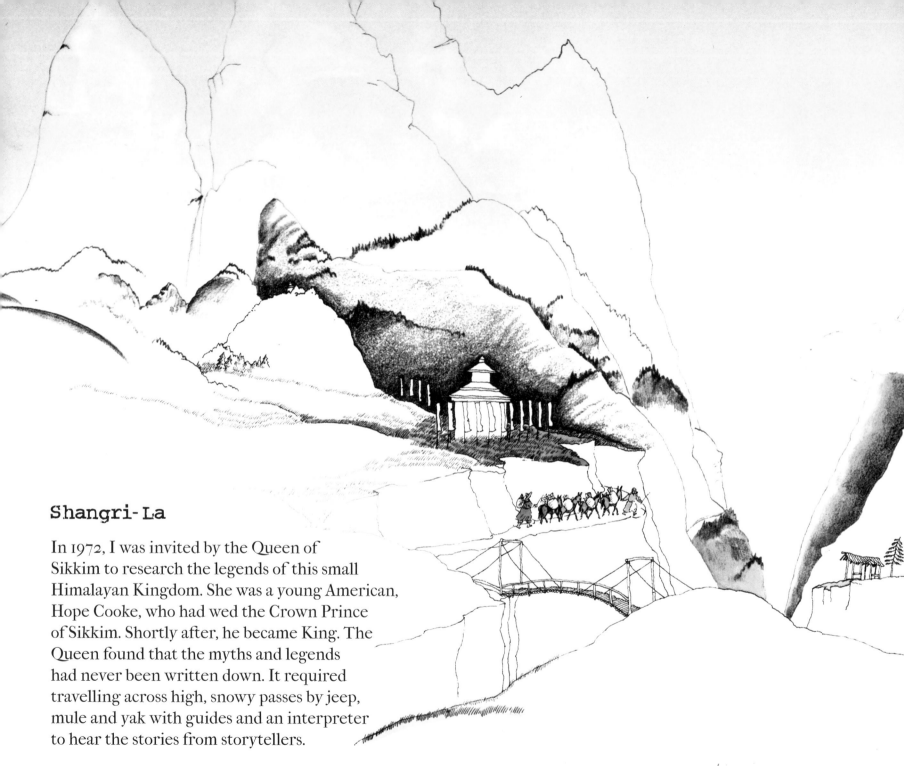

Shangri-La

In 1972, I was invited by the Queen of Sikkim to research the legends of this small Himalayan Kingdom. She was a young American, Hope Cooke, who had wed the Crown Prince of Sikkim. Shortly after, he became King. The Queen found that the myths and legends had never been written down. It required travelling across high, snowy passes by jeep, mule and yak with guides and an interpreter to hear the stories from storytellers.

The mountains are like layer cakes of different climates. Valleys of rushing rivers. Bright waterfalls crash into black pools. Great falling slopes, terraced and green with rice. Corn growing like golden steps to heaven. Dense mossy forests, and higher still, where the sun can penetrate, 600 kinds of orchid, marigolds, and pink cherry blossom peeping through a swirling sea of cloud below, like Hawaiian garlands drifting from a ship.

A pass in the Himalayas, 6km from China

55

After a long twisting journey through the foothills of the Himalayas, we were suddenly above the clouds and there, in the gathering darkness, strung like diamonds around the roof of the world, were the lights of Gangtok, the tiny capital of Sikkim.

The Palace, like a big Swiss chalet with a red tin roof, stood at one end of a plateau. The plateau was ringed by hundreds of tall prayer flags which gave it a joyous and heraldic atmosphere.

Walking with a Queen was a novel experience, especially with everyone dropping to their knees and bumping their foreheads on the ground until we had passed by. It was also very down to earth as monks wandered by, chanting and twirling little prayer wheels and stepping around ducks, chicken and sheep.

Football at The Royal Palace. A cloud blanks out the surrounding valleys and the plateau is an island with its own sun, King and Queen.

Across the valley was the black-forested feet of Mount Kanchenjunga. I didn't notice it for several minutes because I wasn't looking high enough. Its white head was wrapped in a muffler of thick woolly cloud from which, at intervals, rolled a sonorous boom. Was it thunder, or a cracking glacier, or just the noises of a sleeping giant?

Monastery above Lechung, Sikkim, 1972

*Above the valley of Lechung –
the high pass into Tibet*

There followed days of travelling to the north and the high border with Tibet, first by pony and later, as we got higher above the tree line, by yak over swaying wooden bridges and steep snowy tracks.

We stopped just short of the border, and made a lunch of hard-boiled eggs and Nescafé using the yaks as windbreaks, and looked down on the forbidden land of Tibet. We took a trip to find yaks through wonderful forests, first of huge pines and then, a magical dwarf forest, with twisted trees and moss-covered rocks looking like hibernating monsters. The colours were just tipping into autumn.

We climb to 11,000 feet above the tree line to a herd of yaks. We are six kilometres from the Chinese border. We can see Tibet from here. The shaggy yaks grind their teeth thoughtfully as they plod. Loads are roped by frozen, expert fingers before moving off at first light — the stately rhythm of the ancient caravan. The first two hours are bitterly cold. All speech is snatched away by freezing winds.

China via Mongolia

When I first planned to visit China, I couldn't go. At
that time (1974), the country was closed to the world
unless you joined the relevant societies friendly
to China and studied the thoughts and works of
Chairman Mao. I went to meetings and weekend
courses for a couple of years. Eventually, in 1974,
I was allowed to travel to China with a group of trade
unionists, doctors and teachers – about a dozen in all.

As we head down to the Summer Palace by the frozen Kunming lake we see a sequence of richly decorated architecture before ascending the 'Hill of longevity' to the 'Hall that Dispels the Clouds'. We take a short journey to The Ming Tombs Reservoir, past the Statues of Animals leading to the tombs.

The Summer Palace by the frozen Kunming Lake

Back in 1974, Beijing (or Peking as it was then) was a very low-rise city and I could easily see the bulk of my Russian-built hotel rising above the maze of streets. The giant face of Chairman Mao watched from the Forbidden City across the square.

There were of course, no private cars. Wall to wall bicycles, like a blue flood, poured through the streets at rush hour. Wagons pulled by horses, camels and ancient tractors. Smaller carts with towering, teetering burdens were pulled by men and women.

We had to go everywhere in a group, chaperoned by our guides. We visited hospitals, factories, schools and the University of Minorities (there are fifty-four National Minorities in China). There were trips to communes outside the city and, of course, to the Great Wall.

For two days I pretended to be ill, and remained in our hotel until the group had departed on their schedule. Then I wandered the by-ways of the city. I was followed, of course, but I was never approached by my shadows. I didn't want to see or do anything in particular. Just to be part of the crowd. Go with the flow.

Xunhua, North-East China, 1974

Virtually the whole population wore blue. Those who didn't were in the Army. Blue or khaki, the style was the same, the ubiquitous Mao tunic. The more faded and patched the blue, the better. Patches were a sign of hard work and frugality. Old people wore patches on patches.

As we moved north, the climate and conditions became increasingly severe. The blue clothing was padded and many layered.

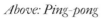

Above: Ping-pong

Top right: Backstreet Blacksmiths and Son

Right: Roadside Chinese chess in the snow

Audience at the Ballet
Northern China '74

Frozen streams.
Boys playing football in icy playground.

visited duck farm.
Old Peoples + Home
Green houses (vegetables staggered stages to ensure supply year round.)
Peoples houses.

All commune members have own plots for self use.
Can keep pigs, chickens goats etc.

Commune members can be sent to industry as needed by State.
Basically use organic fertilizer
Because of nearness to city, most of the land is used for veg.

Old rickshaw man + wife

We visited many homes of industrial workers and villagers. Prize possessions would be a sewing machine and a bicycle for which they had saved long and hard.

The birthplace of Mao was a simple but beautiful farmhouse. To counter rumours at this time about the elderly Mao's poor health, a news report showed him swimming across the Yangtze River. I drew the duck pond where he learned to swim as a boy.

India – Land of Splendour

India never disappoints. The landscape is so vast, so varied; colour, sounds, smells so powerful. The clamour and excitement of the cities, the beauty and tranquillity of the south, and the drama of the high, snowy passes of the North. My first sight of India was in 1972 when I travelled from Delhi to the Himalayas to work on the book of Sikkimese legends. Perhaps the most intense experiences are to be found on the banks of the Ganges.

The Ganges — Benares

An ancient rickshaw man insisted I would be better off with him than in an orthodox taxi. He took me on an unforgettable trundle through indescribable sights and smells to the River Ganges. There he had a friend, a boatman, of course. He took me on a dusk boat trip, oars dipping slowly into the deep green water and little boys bobbing up and down around the boat.

All along one side of the river, the city side, were ranges of steep steps – the ghats. People flooded down these steps, stripped off and plunged into the river. Ladies in brilliant saris bobbed and rose like water lilies.

The heat, the emotion, the multitude of people, the drumming and singing, the ritual of burning bodies – the whole thing was stunning. Flocks of vultures on the opposite bank were doing a spot of beach combing. Probably rich pickings.

The slow inexorable ride home through the hot dark streets was the final sledgehammer to the senses. Cows all over the place. Beautiful little ladies in wonderful colours walking like princesses through the mayhem, babies draped around their necks. And why was I allowing this old man to pedal his guts out to pull me through his own stifling streets to the comfort of my hotel?

Kashmir – Where the Gods Live

I saw much more of India when I returned in 1984, to work with Madhur Jaffrey on her book of Indian Myths and Legends. We travelled by plane over snow-topped mountains, then down into the valley of Kashmir. Our hotel was on a plateau above the glorious Dal Lake. Leaving Madhur in the comfort of the hotel, I set off the next day for Tangmarg, a village in the foothills.

Outside toilets were built facing the roads to encourage passerbys to contribute personal manure. I was happy to oblige – frequently.

My guides hired ponies and we wound our way towards the peak. The snow was now too deep for ponies. Climbing in deep snow is exhausting, particularly when you suddenly sink up to your hip.

Finally, we reached the high plateau. All was silent but for trickling water and the odd crow's cry. The open space after climbing through the forest, the crows circling higher and higher, and the soft pillowy whiteness, entreated us to go on, and on – like a big, inviting, turned-down bed.

Kashmir, Sunday, 15th April

There is a stone hut, and beyond, deep snowfields running upwards towards peaks plumed in cloud. Thunder rolls around. "There may be an avalanche today," says Ashok. I want to go on. But cloud is coming down, and so should we. Going down is worse than going up. It's difficult to stop your feet from running away with you. I am soaked, frozen, glowing! Been where the Gods live.

71

Walking from Village to Village

Wherever I go, I like to walk as much as possible. You are open to the sounds and smells of the place, and you can leave the roads and follow tracks across country. I like experiencing these walks alone – maybe not the whole trip, but days here and there. So it's just you and the place.

In Haryana, the whole flat, dusty land is alive with the coming and going of flocks of sheep, goats and buffalo. At major junctions on main roads there are often snake charmers or small boys with enormous snakes draped around their necks, asking for baksheesh for photos.

Spend the day going to remote villages amongst the backwater of Kerala. When away from the road, after walking across fields for a while, the atmosphere changes, seems timeless. The people, a bit suspicious at first, soon welcome you and are pleased to show you their world.

I walked to the next village in the company of a mahout and his elephant. They travel the countryside entertaining and being fed and sheltered, as do dancing bears, who looked terribly uncomfortable in their fur coats.

73

The Living Arts of Nigeria

Travelling through remote areas of Nigeria in 1972, with the photographer Harri Peccinotti, to research a book about the traditional crafts and artefacts of the people was quite a challenge and, apparently, dangerous at the time due to the number of armed highwaymen, mostly ex-soldiers from the Biafra Civil War.

It was also extremely rewarding. The natural hospitality of the people and the privilege of watching them create such wonderful work using traditional methods and material made this an unforgettable experience.

Above: Dying cloth at Abeokuta

Left: Girl with fruits and goats, and pots piled high ready for firing, at the pottery village of Dawaki near Kano, Northern Nigeria

Different areas of the country specialized in various crafts – wood carving, mask making, weaving and dyeing, pottery, leatherwork, brass and beadwork – depending on tradition and local materials.

Textile village of Abeokuta

Bali - Paradise

I visited Bali in 1974, following a journey through South East Asia. I returned for a longer stay in 1981. It was the nearest thing to paradise. From the sea, rice climbs in steps to the mountains. Volcanoes bury their head in the clouds. Butterflies the size of two hands flapping.

Like steps from Heaven, rice fields mirror the twin streams of work and ritual. Although only men plant rice, both sexes and all ages are involved in the cultivation and harvesting. The building of houses, temples and irrigation systems are all communal duties, and the physical example of the mix of work and art.

Only two hours from Darwin, jumbo jets disgorge tourists daily. Hotel building is restricted to the height of a palm tree and to the southern end of the island around Sanur and Kuta. What effect will the enormous growth of tourism have on Bali? Hopefully less than the effect Bali has on the tourists.

Bamboo scaffolding being carried to Pura Besakih, the Mother Temple of Bali. Renovation work is constantly needed on all the temples, thus traditional skills are perpetuated

Sanur Beach is very popular with the Balinese. After work the beach is crowded with strolling families, bathers and ball players. Hot food is sold from small carts and the tourist frequently comes face-to-face with tradition. The evening procession of ladies, like a box of beautiful coloured pencils, bring offerings to the Gods of fruit, flowers and cakes to float on the retreating tide.

The Universal Language of Football

Football has been a life-long passion. All you need is a ball – the most egalitarian of sports. All over the world, from high in the Andes and Himalayas, to the deserts of Arabia, and the Islands of the South Seas, a bouncing ball is irresistible – especially for me.

I was travelling from Santiago, Chile, into the Andes mountains and came upon a vast landscape of waste from the city. It had been farmland – until the city dumped all its rubbish there. Now, the local people had to 'farm' the rubbish, build with it and recycle it. Naturally, they made space for a football pitch . . .

The school house on the rubbish dump, Chile.
Experiences here inspired my book 'Mia's Story'

In one of the shacks, almost completely dark, except for thin shafts of light from gaps in the roofing, was a small table littered with scraps of vegetable peelings. I thought at first this was a sign of scruffiness, of laziness. Why not clear up after the cooking? I then realised that these peelings had not been discarded — they had been collected from the dumps and were to be the evening meal — a vegetable soup.

Top: *Me playing football in the snow – school yard, Northern China,* 1972. *The children put me in goal and kicked all the balls at me at the same time!*

Above: *South Seas soccer,* 1970

Right: *Football in the City of the Dead, Cairo,* 1986

84

Golan Heights, Israel, 1970. *Seeing children playing football around the world inspired my book* Wonder Goal!

Kuwait, 1979

Yucatan, Mexico, 1979

New York, 1997

Playing with the monks in Sikkim, 1972

Childhood

As the water rat said in *The Wind in the Willows*
– "Believe me, my young friend, there is nothing –
absolutely nothing – half so much worth doing as
simply messing about in boats."

Growing up in a fishing village, with the sea
so much a part of life, with the horizon distant, yet
beckoning, I didn't realize how lucky I was at the time.

We have watched our sons and grandchildren grow
and blossom by the sea and, hopefully, children the
world over, will feel no horizon is too far.

Boats, children fishing – memories of my own childhood

Fisher boys, Philippines

Fishing on Lake Baikal, Siberia

Outrigger – Fiji

The Family of the World

The excitement of travel is, of course, to experience the wonderful variety the world has to offer. A special joy, however, is to witness what we have in common – the love of family, the bond between parent and child.

Home

After a lifetime of travel the most precious memories are of those of home. I liked walking in the woods with our boys and their Grandad. He told us stories, as all Grandad's do, and the falling leaves of autumn reinforced the deep feeling of family and generations to come.

Grandpa and the frog

Of all the journeys, the journey home is always the sweetest –
particularly when it ends in our home in Cornwall.

Nothing can be better than to live at the very end of a railway
at the very end of the country and finally sit with your family
and see the sun slide over the very end of the world.

Rolling home on the train after a round-the-world trip,
down the tunnel of evening into a golden sunset . . .
St Ives spread out in the bay.